Copyright © 2015 by DAVID KILPATRICK

Design and layout: Nathen McVittie

ISBN-10: 0996205802
ISBN-13: 978-0-9962058-0-1

Published by Beadle Books
New York and London

www.beadlebooks.com

Obrigado

A FUTEBOL EPIC

By

David Kilpatrick

Contents

I.	Futebologia
II.	Brazil v Croatia
III.	Mexico v Cameroon
IV.	Spain v Netherlands
V.	Chile v Australia
VI.	Colombia v Greece
VII.	Uruguay v Costa Rica
VIII.	England v Italy
IX.	Côte d'Ivoire v Japan
X.	Switzerland v Ecuador
XI.	France v Honduras
XII.	Argentina v Bosnia-Herzegovina
XIII.	Germany v Portugal
XIV.	Iran v Nigeria
XV.	Ghana v United States
XVI.	Belgium v Algeria
XVII.	Brazil v Mexico
XVIII.	Russia v Korea Republic
XIX.	Australia v Netherlands
XX.	Spain v Chile
XXI.	Cameroon v Croatia
XXII.	Colombia v Côte d'Ivoire
XXIII.	Uruguay v England
XXIV.	Japan v Greece
XXV.	Italy v Costa Rica
XXVI.	Switzerland v France
XXVII.	Honduras v Ecuador
XXVIII.	Argentina v Iran
XXIX.	Germany v Ghana
XXX.	Nigeria v Bosnia-Herzegovina
XXXI.	Belgium v Russia
XXXII.	Korea Republic v Algeria
XXXIII.	United States v Portugal
XXXIV.	Netherlands v Chile
XXXV.	Australia v Spain
XXXVI.	Cameroon v Brazil

XXXVII.	Croatia v Mexico
XXXVIII.	Italy v Uruguay
XXXIX.	Costa Rica v England
XL.	Japan v Colombia
XLI.	Greece v Côte d'Ivoire
XLII.	Nigeria v Argentina
XLIII.	Bosnia-Herzegovina v Iran
XLIV.	Honduras v Switzerland
XLV.	Ecuador v France
XLVI.	Portugal v Ghana
XLVII.	United States v Germany
XLVIII.	Korea Republic v Belgium
XLIX.	Algeria v Russia
L.	Brazil v Chile
LI.	Colombia v Uruguay
LII.	Netherlands v Mexico
LIII.	Costa Rica v Greece
LIV.	France v Nigeria
LV.	Germany v Algeria
LVI.	Argentina v Switzerland
LVII.	Belgium v United States
LVIII.	France v Germany
LIX.	Brazil v Colombia
LX.	Argentina v Belgium
LXI.	Netherlands v Costa Rica
LXII.	Brazil v Germany
LXIII.	Netherlands v Argentina
LXIV.	Brazil v Netherlands
LXV.	Germany v Argentina

Muitíssimo obrigado

Pelé, Dad, Matthew Coppola, Tyler Pittman, Yunus Tuncel, Dean Rader, Jason Barnett, John McDarby, Brian Walsh, Erik Stover, Brenda Elsey, Stanislao Pugliese, Salvatore Cottone, Diane Ackerman, Alison Matika, Kristen Keckler, Khaled AbuNaama, Tim Hall, Paul Steinman, John Hughson, George Quraishi, Michael Agovino, Hossein Fassa, Anthony Guttierez, Eleanora Kupencow, Marshall Dickson

Nathen McVittie for the design and layout

For Lisa, Dylan and Honor

I.
FUTEBOLOGIA: TOWARDS A POETICS OF SPORT

(An Introduction/Methodology/Manifesto/Apology)

64 in 30
Futebol festival – a month takes time outside of time

At consummation I realize:
I've not consumed the Cup
The Cup has consumed me

These principles of moments
Some narrative, some chronicle, reportage
Each game itself a text begging to be read,
Requiring re-presentation
Muthos, ethos, dianoia, lexis, melos, opsis
Tracks for drama, but out of love for language, love for the game I open up
Expose myself to this Muse of Futebolphilia

If eye an ear pretend
If you complain
Or you commend

Blame me not, nor praise me
For though I've courted this Muse
I am but vessel

The game craves word

Martial at the Coliseum
Pausanias at the Games
The player plays his moment
While we watch
We praise to fame
The exposure of the mortal
And perhaps immortal flame
This burning, being burnt

Bodies through space and time
Emerging heroes
Tales to tell
To birth poetic
The passing passes on through sign
Becoming signal
Memories proclaim

II.
BRAZIL v CROATIA
SÃO PAULO

Some sought samba in São Paulo
But after hosts belted their anthem
Three doves sent to flight
And with the three went the dance

Boys in gold at nap
Wake with Marcelo's mishap
Blazers at the hunt

    Is the blood they smell
    In the stadium or the street?

A card to match his shirt
The Hyped One responds
His left to the post to draw level
A sense of some samba revived

And then one ugly moment
Halts beauty's heritage
The cynical, the crass, the dishonest
A dive, a disgrace, as Fred flops

Is this samba
This shift to the left
This stutter forward to the spot
As the Hyped One lucks into the lead?

    Is this blood they smell
    In the stadium or the street?

A ref out of depth
Oscar's toe settles score
Still no samba in São Paulo
More yellow than gold

Dance now
We beg you
For the sake of our love
Bring back the three doves

We have come not for dives
But for dance

III.
MEXICO v CAMEROON
NATAL

Rain in Natal
El Tri quickly robbed
De Santos twice disallowed off

Cameroonian yellow clears
Give the ball back to green
Like Mayans on an ancient court
Care for the ball
Each stroke of a pass a blend
Of risk and security

Can the line not see square through the rain?
The injustice of incompetence
Or the feel of a fix

Sí, se puede
Sí, se puede
A defiant, if ineffectual, roar

Yellow turn golden
The ball loves them now
El Tri betrayed by the hour

And just then

A Mexican rush, slicing diagonal
Deserving Dos Santos but deflects
The pelota's Peralta's
A just twist to the tie

One will do
So three for El Tri

IV.
SPAIN v NETHERLANDS
SALVADOR

El Roja in white
Oranje a dark blue

A soft foul sees the spot for the Champs
And Alonso slips true

Each side press the pitch
To a thin middle third

Til a long ball from Blind
Sent from centre touch

Seeks out a leaping van Persie
His header looping hapless Casillas

The son of a painter
An artist, all the same

Another Blind long Ball
Finds Robben midflight

Foot catch, then a cut
Two pass by til the finish

Here is the samba
A Dutch dream, a dance

Striker-keeper collision
De Vrij picks up the trash

Can revenge for a Final
Be found first round?

Robin's a robber
Iker's pocket picked

Salvador sun turns to rain
As Brazil becomes Happy Holland

Arjen slices through the Armada
And the Dutch dance a samba dream

V.
CHILE v AUSTRALIA
CUIBA

Another red has come to play
The first quarter hour
That's what one would say

But the boy knows the game
Chilean lull, Cahill goal
He says, and it happens

Socceroo physicality
Breaks down Chilean technique
Brave Bravo in goal
Sole Chilean awake

Like them, with them
I drift off
Dull monotony of workman's effort

I dream of art
But he shouts me to wake

One match may seem like many
Put to sleep by too many
Displays of vigorous utility
The drag of physical imposition
Bereft of style

Tired technicians
Burned out ages ago
Denouement before intermission, it seems

Til Beausejour strokes in an addition
And seals the deal

Can fifteen of fun
Justify a dull seventy-five?

I'd just as soon shut my eyes
And dream of masters on the ball

VI.
COLOMBIA v GREECE
BELO HORIZONTE

Hellas' heroes sliced apart from the start
Armero scores and Colombians dance
Cut back opens Hellenic defense
Yellow wave roars its way around
    Belo Horizonte

Defiant blue battle back
With unexpected attack
Gekas heads Hellas' hopes to bar

Teo makes it two
Near post flick to back post poach

If "heroes act like Greeks"
    How Greek is a dive?
Cross bar's cruelty divine retribution

For let it be known:
The gods of play have awakened
And they are aware, they attend
Brasil, this festival

Joga bonito
Or be damned

VII.
URUGUAY v COSTA RICA
FORTALEZA

The brute ugliness of Garra charrúa
Gives Los Ticos an ethical edge

But a white tug of light blue
Puts Cavani to the spot

Le Celeste sweat themselves navy
Black and blue as knocks
They can play but they'd
Much rather fight

Costa Rica strings together
Short pass to pass to pass
    Up the pitch
Until Campbell smashes red to belief

Por suerte Duerte darts at the back
Banana bend to a header
Ureña's first touch lets elegance reign
For at Fortaleza, blue see red

VIII.
ENGLAND v ITALY
MANAUS

Tell me, Gianluca
Is this head over heart?
At the Amazon Arena
All energy England

Don't lose your mind in Manaus
Italians tap to a different tempo

Archetypal 9, Balo heads home Azzurri
Bearded Pirlo's the brain
Leaving Lions white as ghosts
Marking space as blue bodies pass by

No, don't lose your mind in Manaus
Lions might roar another day

IX.
CÔTE D'IVOIRE v JAPAN
RECIFE

Blue Samurai battle Elephant orange
Fans dance their team to a trance
Right the rhythm of play
With the shake of a rattle

Rain falling, Japan open up orange
Like a treasure chest without a lock

A grasshopper hums amidst Elephant play
Drums rattle persistent pressure
And the Samurai gradually give way

X.
SWITZERLAND v ECUADOR
BRASÍLIA

Cheeseheads in the stands
And the Swiss find holes
Less cynical, more strong
"Swiss time was running out…"
To the final tick
Ecuador will never forget

XI.
FRANCE v HONDURAS
PORTO ALEGRE

Anthemless they set to play
So we all miss La Marseillaise
French hit frame
Hondurans hit French
One side resolved to win
One side resolved not to lose

White suffer for their cynicism
Descended as they have in Brasil
The gods of futebol won't endure anti-play

Flash of red at Palacios
Lash from the spot by Benzema

Les Bleus sovereign on the day
In the stands, they break into La Marseillaise
And with song, the game is won

Do eyes deceive
Or is technology true?
With a camera's assist
Les Bleus make it two

The Honduran ten cannot defend
Benzema, blessed this day in Porto Alegre

XII.
ARGENTINA v BOSNIA-HERZEGOVINA
RIO DE JANEIRO

Messi at the Maracanã
Evasive Zbisivic softens the score
But this night in Rio
Just one dancer
Justifies the machine

Semiotic call, so much the Flea
Brave Bosnians cannot stifle such genius
He's simply too quick to kick

So long as Messi does his samba
The enemy within, this Argentine
(Just the one, this 10)
Seems more Brazilian than Brasil

No, no – the Flea plays
    Not like an Argentine
    Not like a Brazilian

No, he plays not like
                    a human
He plays

Must ants work dirt
For this Flea to fly?

XIII.
GERMANY v PORTUGAL
SALVADOR

Portuguese brought their language
Centuries ago to this colonial capital
Today, they didn't bring their futebol

Fröhliche Fußball furthers this neue Deutschland
Disciplined, ja
But drunk on spiel

Müller, majestic, brings memory of Gerd today –
    An opportunist's hattrick –
Brutal, efficient, hungry and proud

XIV.
IRAN v NIGERIA
CURITIBA

No one had noticed
No one had not won or lost
No one had noticed
No game missed a goal

No one will remember
No one was the hero today
Nigerian green and Iranian white
Boos from the bored shower the uninspired

Goalless is no crime
But a game without heroes
Is a workout

XV.
GHANA v UNITED STATES
NATAL

Dream start, a Dempsey dash
Red, white and blue clean through Ghana white
Cut outside right
Cut inside right
Left lets loose – far post
Goal in a blink

Boots on the ground in Brasil

Hamstring clutch, Jozy drops
Unworking threatens unraveling

Is that a shaman in the stands
Some wild traveling witch doctor
Some spell cast to pitch
Battling elements, Ghanians emerge
Like the persistent pulse of an Other

Too familiar to be dehumanized
Personality's emergence
The promise of peripeteia

Boots on the ground in Brasil

Asamoah slices through to Gyan
Who heels to quick Ayew
Past Howard
Two left feet have scored tonight in this goal

Boots on the ground in Brasil
Last gasp corner
Zusi's ball finds a young Berliner
He dreamt this
Shaking his head, this head that sent
Ball to ground then net
He shakes the dream in his head to this real

Boots on the ground in Brasil
Boots on the ground
And dreaming

XVI.
BELGIUM v ALGERIA
BELO HORIZONTE

From the spot, Feghali
With confidence absolute
Patient, he waits movement to shoot
Sure stroke up the middle

Whistles the shrill of cicadas
Serenade each Belgian advance
More and more
Still, Algerian walls show no cracks

Til Fellaini's hair heads backwards
Upper 90
Then Martens blasts to same net space
The Belgians have beat down
Algerian defenses
Bold comeback in Belo sun

XVII.
BRAZIL v MEXICO
FORTALEZA

Memo Ochoa unbeatable
Is Mexico that strong
Or Brasil that weak?

Nil-nil can thrill
If the gods will
Jaguar Ochoa
Shows grace in nullity

XVIII.
RUSSIA v KOREA REPUBLIC
CUIABA

Childlike bobble gifts Korea

Kerzhakov in the box
Turns and pounces like a fox

Two moments of fortune swing balance
Kick this way
         then that
To/o level

XVIX.
AUSTRALIA v NETHERLANDS
PORTO ALEGRE

Robben's brilliant left expected
Cahill's left responds, immediate
He boxes a flag in triumph

But soon an orange stretcher carries Indi off
For Cahill's aggressivity

An unfortunate fist
Gifts Socceroos a spot chance
Jedinek can resist

Brief margin, van Persie brings level
Then just when Australia seem through
Odd chest delivers a dodge from decisive
And Memphis from distance strokes true

Socceroos can't overcome
The brilliance of Oranje in blue

XX.
SPAIN v CHILE
RIO DE JAINERO

Falling Vargas finishes
A series of short diagonals
Down the Spaniards' left flank

An Alonso error exposes El Roja
And Aránguiz blasts the champions
To an early exit

Chileans charging ticketless
Through the Maracanã's media wall
Sequestered in Rio
They'll still say they were there

Too late for tiki taka
Sloppy Spain ashamed
By the charging Chileans
Forcing abdication

XXI.
CAMEROON v CROATIA
MANAUS

Song sees red
His elbow hammer
Smash into Mandžukić's back
Bizarre blow to Indomptables

Blazers make Lions
Look like kittens

XXII.
COLOMBIA v CÔTE D'IVOIRE
BRASÍLIA

Tactically tight, tense level
Til James Rodríguez rises above Drogba
And Los Cafeteros samba as one

James steals at midfield
Quintero slots through
Waking Elephants

Gervinho twists through from left touch
To keep it a contest
But Drogba blows two chances

Los Cafeteros hold on
James rising
This birth of a star in Brasília

XXIII.
URUGUAY v ENGLAND
SÃO PAULO

Suárez finds space and heads home
Rooney blasts straight to keep
A life can come down to such a chance
Given another, he touches true to level
And I see chariots of fire
Ablaze through the São Paulo sky
Suddenly Suárez breaks free
The ball finds him in stride
Off the head of Stevie G
Training ground familiar
Were it not country but club
Lightning flash of Suárez triumphant
Garra charrúa to the whistle

XXIV.
JAPAN v GREECE
NATAL

No heroics from Hellas
Red shown
For white recklessness
Reduces the game to a slog
Blue Samurai can't break Greeks down
Though down a man
A draw is not a win

XXV.
ITALY v COSTA RICA
RECIFE

Balo bragged he'd kiss the Queen
While Lion dreams relied
But turn of an ankle when clean through
Sees Balo's shot go wide
Then twice his chance denied

Ticos have not bought the hype
Ruiz from the right heads under bar
Line crossed Azzurri stunned

Pirlo wastes a free into the wall
Door bolted shut
Had Italy taken the lead
Instead
Ticos not so cynical
High lines pushed to please
Eyes divine fixed at Recife

Though passing and possession
Azzurri dominate
One chance is all you need
To earn a goddess' kiss

XXVI.
SWITZERLAND v FRANCE
SALVADOR

Giroud climbs, lifting les Bleus
Poking holes in Swiss defense

Pantheon of Platini, Zidane, Henry
Welcome Benzema as new Sun King

Les Bleus run riot through the reds
Gallic glory at la foot restored

After ceding five to the French
Two consolations soften Swiss shame

XXVII.
HONDURAS v ECUADOR
CURITIBA

Long, long ball sent one third to another
Costly – chest, touch, run and smash
Two blasts from box to net
Route one, one goal

But Honduran hearts quickly crushed
Valencia strides behind a flat white four for a tap
Then off a free he rises
His nod to net unleashes Ecuadoran voice

Sing to the final whistle
Sing a victory song

Ball slipped beneath his shirt
Valencia kisses like a mother her baby

XXVIII.
ARGENTINA v IRAN
BELO HORIZONTE

For ninety minutes
Iranians red as stop lights
Just one magic moment

The left boot of Messi bends the ball
Around two lunging defenders
Past outstretched Haghighi

Inside far post, net rippling
Seconds of genius
Trump an hour and a half of discipline

XXIX.
GERMANY v GHANA
FORTALEZA

Fortaleza heat sets a slow pace
Both sides strong but patient
Trading tests

Billed as the Boateng brothers' battle
Germany send Jérôme off first
Shed of sibling storyline
The match finds life

Götze's header-knee from Müller's cross
A bounce Dauda cannot find

The Prince comes off
And Andre Ayew
Joined by his brother a moment before
Rises about the Big F'n, Per
Header for header
Ghanian gall sees Gyan smash

But a yard's Klose range
To level again

Bloodied Müller and Boye
On their backs at the whistle
Level on ground and tally

Given all, draw's fair
Both played without fear
For gods' approval

XXX.
NIGERIA v BOSNIA-HERZEGOVINA
CUIABA

Džeko clean through from Pjanić
False flag renders null and void
A blown call's but a blink
But rather no call than wrong
One might think
Until his opposite line ignores
Emeneke turning Spahić to ground
Then cutting back for Odemwingie
Nigerians drop, content to coast and counter
Two calls, one goal, that's game

XXXI.
BELGIUM v RUSSIA
RIO DE JANEIRO

Red Devils dancing in the stands
Origi is their man
Eden the spark
Tactical tension stalemating
Eden breaks through to the by
Then cuts back
                    to pick out
Origi is the man
Space enough in Russia's belly
Turn, blast – back of the net
Belgium is through

Play that way the whole game, Devils
Perhaps we'll dance with you

XXXII.
KOREA REPUBLIC v ALGERIA
PORTO ALEGRE

The Desert Foxes tear apart
Red Tigers with aplomb
Pedestrian, predictable, without spark
Nothing more than a work ethic
Algerians snip, snip, snip away

XXXIII.
UNITED STATES v PORTUGAL
MANAUS

So much to prove
Early going gaffe
Cameron slices in his box
A gift to Nani
Reinforces Yank critique
Precompetent technique

Still guts and grit, no quit

Just past an hour
Jermaine Jones lets rip a bending blast
Beto can only watch this strike sublime

Dempsey's belly goal closer to type
Time ticking on this test
A point's been proven
                              but
Last gasp feels like fate:
                        Bradley
                         Eder
                         Nani

Ronaldo

                                                       Varela

                             Finis

XXXIV.
NETHERLANDS v CHILE
SÃO PAULO

Both teams already advanced
Each has to decide
To bore or to dance
Tactical teasing
Each chances a thrill
Will genius emerge
With a goal for the kill?
Dutch defer to Chilean verve
But Sanchez denied
Sub Fer's first touch
A header goal
Truce broken, final flourish
Robben's racing knows only full tilt
Memphis keeps the pace, finds space
And wins the race for Oranje
Two subs, two goals, two survivors

XXXV.
AUSTRALIA v SPAIN
CURITIBA

As if mourning lost glory
Spain wear black, not red
They've read their obituary
Abdication comes with regal resignation
Villa step over heel flick
Torres tuck
Mata meg
Brilliance bereft of competitive edge
Grants ceremonial egress
Humble half-celebrations like waves goodbye

XXXVI.
CAMEROON v BRAZIL
BRASÍLIA

Nyom, already yellowed
Shoves the Hyped One
No second card
Neymar's next touch hits net

The boys in gold are back
Here is the joy – jogo bonito

Cameroonian green and red
Has an accent of gold
Not enough to stop the samba
Three games in, now clicking
The boys in gold are back home

XXXVII.
CROATIA v MEXICO
RECIFE

Rafa heads El Tri ahead
Guardado makes it two
Then Chicharito makes it three for El Tri

Late Rakitić to Perišić sends Vatrani away with small consolation

These Mexicans play with verve, flash and fight
How far away from Mayan ball court
Yet how close to their passionate play

XXXVIII.
ITALY v URUGUAY
NATAL

Down a man, needing but a draw
Prandelli hedges Azzurri hopes
Lock for lock
Five at back to five at back
Chip, knock, slog – little craft

Chiellini al dente
Once again mad Suárez reveals
The hunger at the heart of garra Charrúa
Bite unpunished on the pitch
Marks on shoulder as red as Marchisio's card

A moment after treachery allowed
The ball bounces off the back of Godín's head

Italy exit
Ironically white Celeste move on
Again, at game's expense

Pray the gods will not reward
Joga bonito or be damned
Garra Charrúa be damned

Say something Galeano
You prophet to a barren land
Too much in shadow

XXXIX.
COSTA RICA v ENGLAND
BELO HORIZONTE

Ticos proud, already through
Lions tamed, vacation's due
Not much left to do
But draw
No ambition for spectacle
Nil-nil a bore

Why kick the ball?

XL.
JAPAN v COLOMBIA
CUIABÁ

Maya Yoshida spins like a top
James with ball at pace
Then flips the ball
Over helpless Kawashima

Cosmetic or beside the point
Why four when two will do?

No, Los Cafeteros are here to play
Golden joy in Cuiabá
Colombia's birthed a star

XLI.
GREECE v CÔTE D'IVOIRE
FORTALEZA

Samaris walls through with Samaras
Gervinho feeds Wilfried
Elephants look through
Til Samaras steps to the spot
Late rescue more luck than heroic

XLII.
NIGERIA v ARGENTINA
PORTO ALEGRE

Not yet three minutes
Messi roofs
But Musa needs little more than a minute
And Super Eagles equalize

At the edge of half
Messi magic from a free

Just after break, Super Eagles slice through
Musa once more

Roja's knee at fifty, from corner
Proves enough for La Albiceleste

XLIII.
BOSNIA-HERZEGOVINA v IRAN
SALVADOR

Princes of Persia starving for glory
Patient Dragons wait for break
Džeko won't be denied by post
Switch from besieged to storming
Won't suit such Šāhzādegāne
Stars dim to Dragons as Pjanić slots home
Already eliminated
Goal Ghoochannejhad slight solace
No chance to push on
Bosnians play free

Both go with grace, pride restored

XLIV.
HONDURAS v SWITZERLAND
MANAUS

Left upper 90
Tuck low right
Then left
Shaqiri strikes thrice
Swiss flattered by score
Los Catrachos exposed from bravado

XLV.
ECUADOR v FRANCE
RIO DE JANEIRO

Gallic pride already restored
Les Bleus in white easily withstand
These yellow shirts
Faces tucked inside
Conceding the bitter truth
They haven't the feet for the dance

XLVI.
PORTUGAL v GHANA
BRASÍLIA

Boye knees to his own upper 90
But Gyan's head brings Ghana level

Cash flown, content
They play with intent
Despite slim chance of survival
From this brutal Group of Death

Ronaldo misses and misses
Til Duada spikes down
This time the Portuguese prince hits for net

Enough for today
Some hint of pride
But not enough for either side
Ghana gone, the Portuguese go with them

XLVII.
UNITED STATES v GERMANY
RECIFE

These countries, these cousins
In rainy Recife
To draw is no disgrace
Last time, a draw felt like defeat
This time, a loss feels like a win
Five Yanks German born
Klinsmann both kin and kind

Howard clears Mertesacker's header to Müller
Who takes his chance with aplomb

Late Yank miss of no consequence
These cousins have already survived
To play another day
Such loss is no disgrace

XLVIII.
KOREA REPUBLIC v BELGIUM
SÃO PAULO

Defour sees red before the break
For stamping Shin-wook's shin
This Belgian ten need just a chance
Seung-gyu stops Duock Origic's drive
But Vertonghen pounces clear for win
Red Devils in black book a date with the States

XLIX.
ALGERIA v RUSSIA
CURITIBA

Desert Foxes down when Kombarov crosses to Kokorin
Hosting on horizon, Russians desperate to prove their game
But on the hour, late Slimani heads
Algeria level and through

L.
BRAZIL v CHILE
BELO HORIZONTE

The Hyped One approaches the spot
His shift left, his stutter forward
A dance we've seen before
Legacy on his shoulders
Neymar keeps his nerve for net
Jara plants pitch but strikes bar
The gods have rescued the hosts
And the party goes on
Scolari lifts the Hyped One
Tears flowing, like a father
Embracing his son
To fight on
Crazy things happen in Belo Horizonte
But do us a favor, we implore
Dance us some samba, then let's dance some more

It is not enough
Just to win
Joga bonito or be damned

LI.
COLOMBIA v URUGUAY
RIO DE JANEIRO

Al dente absence leaves warriors
Up for a fight
While Colombian gold seems native
True and pure
Head to head to chest
                          volley
                                    goal
James, a star, rising
James triumphs at the dance

LII.
NETHERLANDS v MEXICO
FORTALEZA

Rafa steps on Robben's foot
A dive to survive
Mexican misfortune
Dutch delight

LIII.
COSTA RICA v GREECE
RECIFE

"The end's the same"
Not keen to know, I say
"Hell no"
We watch the ball
I tell him Greeks are wearing blue
Remind him Italy were robbed
He nods
Staring at the screen
Hospitaled, 85 at 90 needs rest
So we race another screen to see
Ticos take Hellas from spot
Added time heroics only an extension –
The end's the same

LIV.
FRANCE v NIGERIA
BRASÍLIA

Moses clears the line from Benzema
And Cabaye crashes bar
Spectacular Enyeama saves Super Eagles time and again
Til he palms to Pogba's head

Late Yobo own no matter
Les Bleus end Eagles' flight

LV.
GERMANY v ALGERIA
PORTO ALEGRE

An anti-futebol memory
Anschluß at Gijón
Fuels Fenneas' flames

Müller slips while Neuer sweeps to extra
Schürrle's left heel flicks behind his right
Then Özil blasts relief
Djabou volleys Desert Foxes late consolation

Die Mannschaft no machine
All-too-human this will-to-win

LVI.
ARGENTINA v SWITZERLAND
SÃO PAULO

118 minutes of apprehension
Then Messi bursts –
A skip, a jump, a touch
Left foot to the diagonal right
DiMaria needs just one touch, one chance
But Swiss not broken
So close, the post, imbalanced deflection
Still one more chance
A free inside the D
The wall holds to whistle
Swiss time's run out
Flea saves Albiceleste again
To play another day

Please don't wait so long
Or your luck may see you wronged

LVII.
UNITED STATES v BELGIUM
SALVADOR

The first of sixteen, Howard saves opening minute
Jersey boy, tattooed warrior
No more talk of Tourette's
He has overcome, transformed heroic
But the gods of futebol demand more than the keeper's "no"
One must win
Wave after wave, Devils denied
And at the edge of full
The chance we all dream of
Falls to Wondolowski
Six yards out, skying high, he fails
A nightmare miss to live with
One must win
The boys battle on
Boots on the ground in Brazil
Fresh Lukaku too much to bear
Breaks down Uncle Sam's barrier
With a ball to De Bruyne
Who returns favor to take it to two
Golden goal sudden death would spare collapse
Another quarter-hour embarrassment threat
Then long distance Bradley at last
Shows more than rugged tenacity
Precision chip, jung Green volleys home
Still believe, no surrender
The Yankees are on the attack
Is there enough time, enough strength, to comeback?
Technique unconcealed with unshackled verve
Last chance set piece choreography dazzles Devils
But Deuce can't make deuce dying seconds
Disappointing Devils far from heroes today
A nation awake with belief
Ah – you need feet for this dance
Do – dare for the gods' delight!
Boots on the ground, but
One must win

LVIII.
GERMANY v FRANCE
RIO DE JANEIRO

The Germans celebrate
As if they beat the French
Set piece a dozen in
But ball to Deutscher kopf
Nudging out slack Les Bleus
Neither side kissed by a Muse
They slog on and on
Til Benzema gets his break, late
    Down the left
Smash upper near to
Neuer's hand
Traffic cop austerity reflex
No!

This did not seem an elimination
No Franco-Prussian War
But just the same
The Germans celebrate
As if they beat the French

LIX.
BRAZIL v COLOMBIA
FORTALEZA

I miss the blue shorts of Brasil
Though Los Cafeteros have been more golden
Home yellow force Colombia red

Joga bonito or be damned

The football finds
Thiago's thigh
The golden ring roars

But Brasil betray heritage
Beneath its very strain
Brilliant James hounded and harried by foul Fernandinho

Joga bonito or be damned

Foul after foul
Some called but no cards for caution
Til James earns for a trifle

Joga bonito or be damned

Sins for their damnation
James hacked too many times
Zúñiga knees Hype down to send Neymar

Stretchered to the sky
Damned souls taste bitter victor's wine
Victors but not vintage

LX.
ARGENTINA v BELGIUM
BRASÍLIA

Studied if uninspired

The Flea receives, spins – finds space
Devils ought not be so lax
He slices the ball through
Deflection falls to Higuaín
This is all the magic we will see
This studied workshift
Messidependencia requires just a moment
Offered another, the Flea is swatted aside
He's done enough, again

Had Lukaku the nerve
Belgium might offer a dose of drama
But this early flash of skill from luck
Is all Argentine students require

LXI.
NETHERLANDS v COSTA RICA
SALVADOR

Dutch chance after chance
Flags off more than on
Just one late Tico chance

White Ticos on their knees
Proud Oranje on their feet
Two hours scoreless
Set up this spot test
Fate left to the gods

Krul confidence leaves Ticos
On their knees

LXII.
BRAZIL v GERMANY
BELO HORIZONTE

No golden 10
Broken back of the Hyped One
Dominating babble

Another deafening anthem shout
Die Mannschaft calm in the soundstorm

Off the corner all alone
This Müller's tale, a kiss home
Lethal beauty from surgical precision
The blitzkrieg's just begun

The gods of futebol exact bitter revenge
For Brasil's betrayal of jogo bonito
Boos shower down at the damned full anthem volume by half
Transformed Germans better embody the ideal
Brazilian tears rain in Belo Horizonte
No golden 10
A beat back for bullyball

This yellow eleven must change

LXIII.
NETHERLANDS v ARGENTINA
SÃO PAULO

Tense and tentative til late
Robben takes a touch too many, twice
For all the Messidependencia
No magic moment grants escape
Studied solid Argentines show rare daring
Palacio through – rushed header
A last chance for full-play heroics
Spot tactics tricksters out of tricks
Some karma carries Argentines to Final

LXIV.
BRAZIL v NETHERLANDS
BELO HORIZONTE

This game should not be played
Say so many
From Der Kaiser to van Gaal
If only pride is on the line
Hosts have much to play for

But they start where they left off

Torn apart by Dutch precision
Flat-footed, following play
Not dictating

Having lived by the sword, deserving
Punishment from futebol gods
They sold their sporting soul
Now pay the price

No jogo bonito, so damned

LXV.
GERMANY v ARGENTINA
RIO DE JANEIRO

Man v machine a mantra for Maracanã
Color omen brings split to mind
But for all the myth and tradition
Diese neue deutscher Fußball too fluid for the stereotype
Winning tradition, both
But if the dancing divines
Who have spent the month in samba reverie
Reward the month's play, white will win

Higuaín gifted through but wastes left
Harder to miss
What god guides aside?
A second chance he finishes, but off
The lifted flag suspending celebration
Höwedes header hammers off post at half whistle

Messi through left – a miss right
Golden sky on Cristo Redentor
The Cup has no value
Yet more prized than any objet d'art
The world is watching
More than ever
Now
One in focus
One object – the ball
For another – the cup
Time ticking, slowing as genius anticipation wearies
Weakness, some failure exploited more likely
One must win
Something must give
It will
But when?
They say, just put it on the frame
Unless, you just put it on the frame
After 90, no hero, play on

Pony-tailed Palacio misses left and again
Harder to miss
What god guides aside?
Maschereno, already yellowed, mugs Schweinsteiger
Still 7 soldiers

Fifteen minutes left
The world watching
This sacred moment of unified focus global
Begs a hero

Bloodied Schweinsteiger battles but
The gods give us Götze, a goal
One more chance for Messi magic
Wasted over bar

Argentine tears at Maracanã
The end's the same
Tears of all the nations flow together to one stream

Gods assured
The best team has won

www.ingramcontent.com/pod-product-compliance
Lightning Source LLC
Chambersburg PA
CBHW031428290426
44110CB00011B/580